wackycakes
&kookycookies

wackycakes
&kookycookies

Gerhard Jenne   photography by Jonathan Lovekin

BARNES & NOBLE

NEW YORK

Text copyright © 1998, 2006 Gerhard Jenne
Design and photographs copyright
© 1998, 2006 Ryland Peters & Small

This 2006 edition published by Barnes & Noble
Publishing Inc. by arrangement with Ryland Peters
& Small Inc.

2006 Barnes & Noble Publishing

ISBN-13: 978-0-7607-8287-3
ISBN-10: 0-7607-8287-3

A CIP catalog record for this book is available
from the Library of Congress.

Printed in China.

1 3 5 7 9 10 8 6 4 2

Publishing Director **Anne Ryland**

Designer **Sally Powell**

Art Assistant **Sailesh Patel**

Project Editor **Maddalena Bastianelli**

Editors **Anne Hildyard, Elsa Petersen-Schepelern**

Stylist **Wei Tang**

Food Stylist **Gerhard Jenne**

Production **Meryl Silbert**

Illustrator **Michael Hill**

Author Photograph **Jonathan Lovekin**

contents

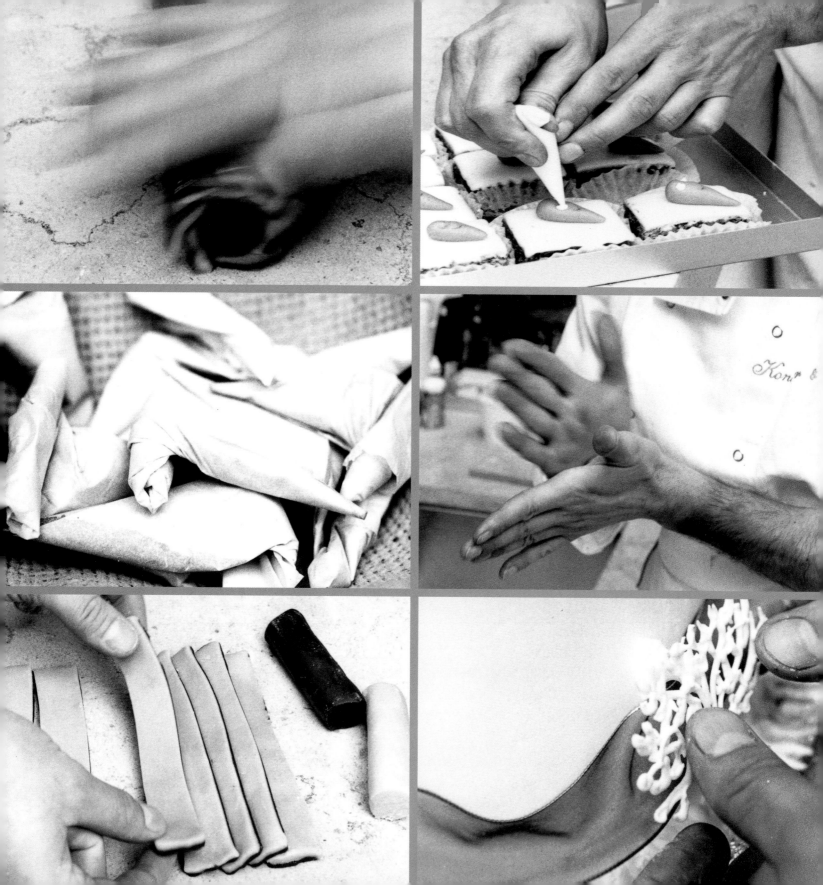

introduction

Decorating cakes and cookies is a fun and rewarding experience. You don't have to be an experienced pastry chef—or even particularly artistic. You just need a sense of humor and a steady hand!

But no matter how beautiful the final decoration, I believe passionately that my creations must taste terrific. So—you will find that this book opens with good, basic recipes for delicious cakes and cookies, plus others for fillings and frostings.

When it comes to decoration, most of my techniques are really quite simple. You don't need expensive equipment —just parchment paper, a few sharp knives, sheets of thick plastic, and a rolling pin.

You don't have to follow my designs to the letter—use your imagination, and have fun!

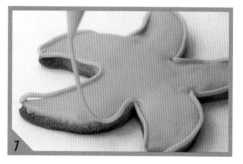

techniques

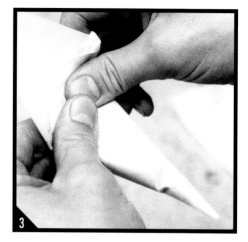

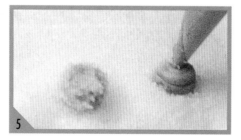

1 To make a paper piping bag, cut a 10-inch square of parchment paper diagonally into two triangles. Hold the long side of one triangle in your left hand, grasp one corner with the other and roll to make a cone shape. Repeat with the other corner, so the 2 points meet. Fold the flap inside to secure.

2 Fill the bag with royal icing without letting it touch the top of the bag.

3 Push the icing down towards the tip of the bag, then roll the paper over to seal.

4 To make colored royal icing, transfer some icing to a board or bowl. Add a few drops of food coloring and mix with a palette knife.

5 To make bobbles or stamens, build royal icing to shape by piping into sugar.

6 Create a zig-zag effect by moving the piping bag from side-to-side while piping.

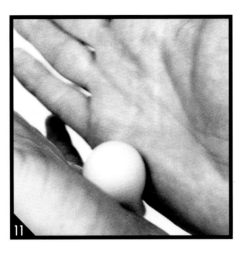

7 To pipe close to the edge of the cookie or cake, keep the bag upright.

8 To make stamens, pipe short curved lines.

9 To work marzipan, roll it between 2 sheets of thick plastic.

10 To raise shapes, pipe icing underneath.

11 To make balls of marzipan, roll a small piece between your palms.

12 Use a ball to shape an elephant's head.

13 Flatten smaller marzipan balls for the ears.

14 Dab or stipple a cat cookie with melted chocolate to resemble fur.

15 Add scraped chocolate for thicker fur-effect.

filling, frosting, and decorating

Chocolate Ganache

Created in Paris by the Pâtisserie Siraudin in the 1850s, this rich chocolate cream is used to fill and cover cakes, to make chocolate truffles, and decorate desserts.

1 cup unsweetened chocolate, chopped
1 cup light cream
Makes 1⅓ cups

Put the chocolate in a bowl set over a saucepan of hot (not simmering) water and melt gently. Alternatively, microwave it on medium power for 1–2 minutes, stirring every 30 seconds until melted. Put the cream into a small saucepan and bring to a boil.
1 Pour the hot cream over the melted chocolate.
2 Using a wooden spoon, stir well to form a lump-free mixture. Beat until smooth and glossy. Cool.

Homemade Almond Paste

One of the most important pâtisserie preparations, almond paste is used to cover and decorate cakes.

2½ cups ground almonds
3 cups confectioner's sugar
3 medium egg yolks
juice of ½ lemon
1 tablespoon brandy
Makes 1½ lb.

Put all the ingredients in a food processor, then work to a firm paste, like freshly made pastry. Briefly knead until smooth, wrap in plastic and chill until required.

Chocolate

Melted chocolate can be used for piping simple decorations. Fill the paper piping bag with 2 oz. of melted chocolate, seal, trim the tip, and pipe onto cakes, cookies, or parchment paper. Work with small amounts of chocolate so the piping is easier to control.

Lemon Chiffon Frosting

A tangy frosting ideal as a filling and topping for rich cakes—the oils from the lemon zest produce a strong citrus flavor, and the yellow flecks are very attractive.

4 cups confectioner's sugar
1 cup cream cheese
grated zest and juice of 1 lemon
4 tablespoons sweet butter,
    melted and cooled
Makes 3⅓ cups

Put the confectioner's sugar, cream cheese, lemon zest, and juice in a food processor and blend until smooth. Add the butter and blend again. If the mixture is too soft, add a little extra confectioner's sugar. After chilling, the frosting will set harder.

Quick Butter Frosting

A light, creamy frosting, plain or flavored, that can be be used as a filling and covering for cakes. It is endlessly versatile—add a splash of brandy or rum for a special treat.

1 cup sweet butter, softened
2 cups confectioner's sugar, sifted
flavorings such as vanilla extract, lemon
    or orange zest, or ½ cup unsweetened
    chocolate, melted (optional)
Makes 2⅓ cups chocolate
frosting, or 2 cups other flavors

Put the butter in a bowl and, using a wooden spoon or electric mixer, beat until creamy. Gradually beat in the confectioner's sugar until the mixture is white and fluffy. Add flavoring, if using, and stir well.

frostings for decorating

Royal Icing

Royal icing is undoubtedly the king of frostings and has always been the classic choice for wedding or Christmas cakes. It is particularly well suited for piping decorations, and is also ideal for inscribing cakes and cookies or for making sugar ornaments. Add glycerine (available from drugstores) to soften the mixture before using.

3 medium egg whites
juice of ½ lemon
6½–7½ cups confectioner's sugar, sifted
2 teaspoons glycerine (optional)
Makes 2¼–3¼ cups
(enough to cover and decorate one 8-inch cake)

Put the egg whites, lthe emon juice and half the sifted confectioner's sugar into a large bowl. Stir with a wooden spoon until creamy (do not beat, or air pockets will form in the mixture.) Gradually stir in the remaining sugar until the mixture is white and smooth. Lift the spoon out of the bowl to test the consistency—it should be glossy and form soft peaks. Add the glycerine, if using.

Royal icing can be made in advance, then kept in the refrigerator for several days in an airtight container. Cover the surface with plastic, stretch a damp cloth over the top, and cover with a lid. Chill until required. Before using, stir well, and if necessary add more sifted confectioner's sugar.

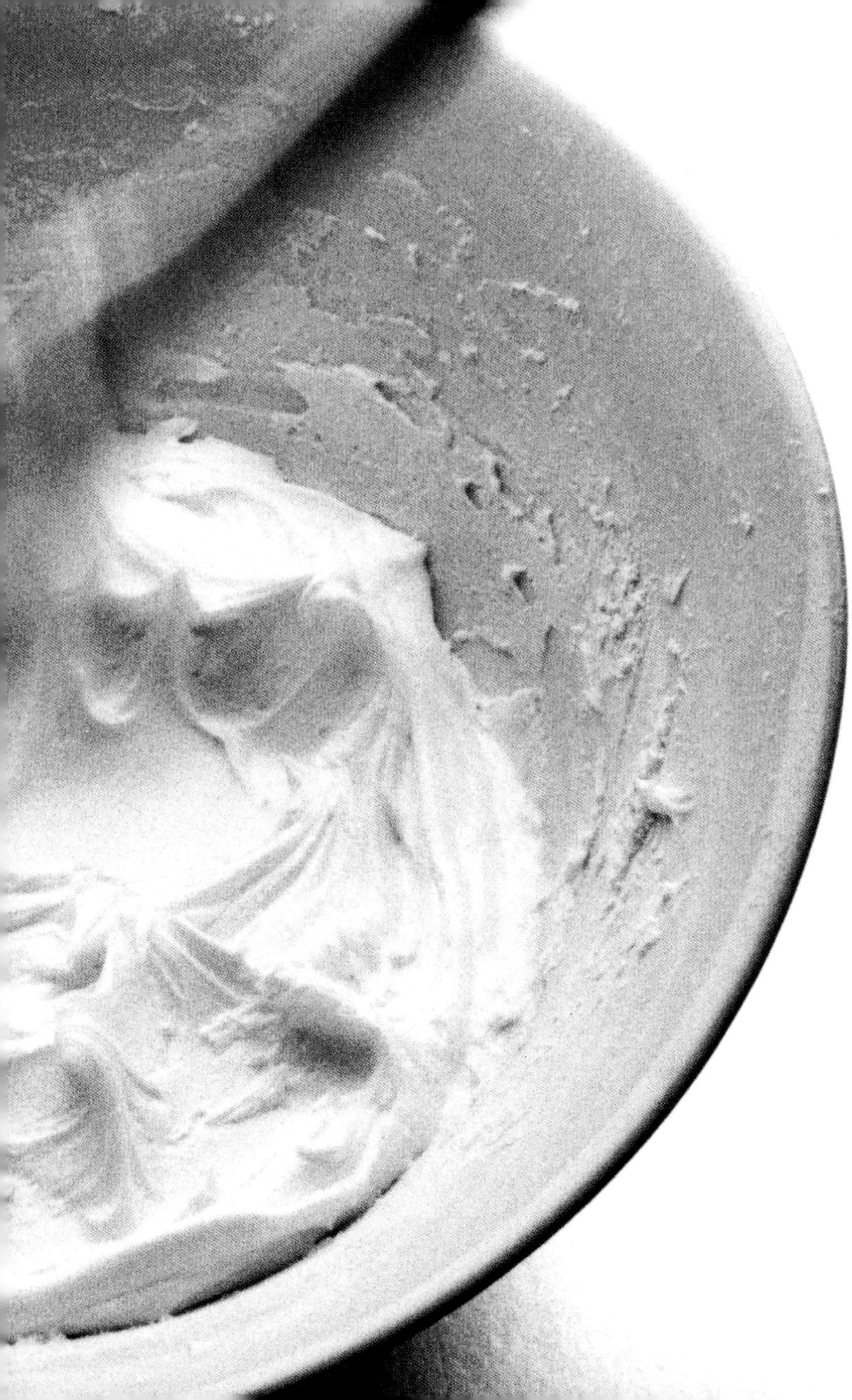

Fondant Frosting

Making fondant is a very complex process, best left to professionals. A short-cut is to buy it ready-made from a supermarket, then melt it with lemon juice to give a flowing consistency for coating.

⅔ cup ready-made fondant frosting
juice of ½ lemon
Makes about 1 cup

Melt the fondant and lemon juice in a small pan over a low heat. (Lemon juice enhances flavor and takes the edge off the sweetness.) Stir constantly until the temperature reaches 130°F and test carefully with the back of a finger. Do not overheat or the fondant will lose its sheen.

Lemon Water Frosting

A useful alternative to fondant. The mixture is shiny when first made, but soon loses its gloss, so make it just before use.

3 cups confectioner's sugar, sifted
juice of 1 lemon, strained
1 tablespoon cold water
Makes 1⅓ cups

Put the confectioner's sugar and lemon juice in a food processor and blend until creamy and smooth. Add more juice or sugar, if necessary, to alter the consistency. To stop a crust forming, store the frosting in an airtight container.

decorating cookies

If you've never tried cake decorating before, decorating cookies is a great way to start. Baking them is infinitely simpler and cheaper than tackling a full-scale wedding or birthday cake and you can develop your decorating skills on a small scale. All the cookies in this chapter are decorated in great detail, but they can also be made in simpler styles.

When you've finished your artistic endeavors, presentation is half the battle—package them in a colorful box, on a beautiful plate, or gift-wrapped and tied with a smart ribbon. You can also sandwich wafer-thin cookies together with lemon curd, jam, or Quick Butter Frosting (page 10) before decorating them in the exciting ways shown here.

basic recipes for cookies

Vanilla Sablés

1¼ cups confectioner's sugar, sifted
½ teaspoon vanilla extract
1 medium egg yolk
1 cup plus 2 tablespoons salted butter, diced
2½ cups all-purpose flour, sifted
2 oz. unsweetened chocolate, to decorate
Makes about 30 cookies

Put the sugar, vanilla, egg yolk and butter in a bowl and mix quickly together with your fingers or a wooden spoon. Add the flour and mix to a firm dough, working as fast as possible, especially in hot temperatures—if it becomes oily the finished cookies will shrink and harden. Shape the dough into a flat slab, wrap and chill for 1 hour or up to 1 week.

When ready to bake, roll out on a floured surface to ⅛ inch thick. Cut out rounds with a 3-inch cookie cutter. Place apart on lightly buttered baking trays and cook in a preheated oven at 400°F for 12 to 14 minutes until golden. Remove from the oven and let cool on a wire rack. Serve immediately, or add piped patterns with melted chocolate (page 10) . Let set before serving.

Chocolate Sablés

1¼ cups confectioner's sugar, sifted
1 medium egg yolk
1 cup plus 2 tablespoons salted butter, diced
2¼ cups all-purpose flour, sifted
½ cup unsweetened cocoa powder, sifted
2 oz. unsweetened chocolate, to decorate
Makes about 30 cookies

Make the dough in the same way as for vanilla sablés. Alternatively, put all the ingredients in a food processor, blend briefly, switch off the machine and scrape down the sides with a spatula. Blend again to form a dough. Shape into a flat slab, wrap in plastic and chill for about 1 hour or up to 1 week.

When ready to bake, roll out the dough on a floured surface to ⅛ inch thick. Cut out rounds with a 3-inch cookie cutter. Place apart on lightly buttered baking trays and cook in a preheated oven at 400°F for 12 to 14 minutes. Lift a cookie off the baking tray: if the base is cooked it will lift off easily. Remove from the oven and let cool on a wire rack. Pipe decorative patterns with melted chocolate (page 10) and let set before serving.

Stem Ginger Cookies

1 piece preserved stem ginger, finely chopped
2 tablespoons syrup from the jar of preserved ginger
6 tablespoons superfine sugar
½ cup plus 2 tablespoons salted butter, diced
1½ cups all-purpose flour, sifted
2 oz. unsweetened chocolate, to decorate
Makes about 20 cookies

Put the stem ginger in a bowl with the ginger syrup from the same jar, and the sugar. Stir with a wooden spoon, then mix in the butter. Gradually add the flour, work to a dough with your fingers, then knead until the dough is smooth and firm. Shape into a flat slab, wrap in plastic, and chill for 1 hour or up to 1 week.

When ready to bake, roll out the dough on a floured surface to about ⅛ inch thick. Using a sharp knife, cut out freehand shapes or cut rounds using a 3-inch cookie cutter. Place apart on several lightly buttered baking trays and cook in a preheated oven at 350°F for 13 to 15 minutes. Remove from the oven and cool on a wire rack. Pipe decorative patterns with melted chocolate (page 10) and let set before serving.

Gingerbread

¾ cup brown sugar

4 tablespoons light corn syrup (or golden syrup)

2 tablespoons dark corn syrup (or black treacle)

2 teaspoons ground cinnamon

2 teaspoons ground ginger

a pinch of ground cloves

grated zest of 1 orange

¾ cup salted butter, diced

1 teaspoon baking soda, sifted

2⅔ cups all-purpose flour, sifted

Makes about 34 cookies

Put the sugar, both corn syrups, cinnamon, ginger, cloves, orange zest, and 2 tablespoons water in a small saucepan. Bring to a boil, stirring. Remove from the heat and stir in the butter, until melted. Add the baking soda. Stir in the flour while the mixture is warm. Turn out the dough, wrap, and chill for 1 hour or up to 1 week.

When ready to bake, roll out the dough on a lightly floured surface to about ⅛ inch thick. Cut rounds with a 3-inch cookie cutter, or shapes using templates (page 78). Place the cookies apart on several baking trays lined with parchment paper. Cook in a preheated oven at 350°F for 13 to 15 minutes. Remove from the oven and let cool on the baking trays for 5 minutes. Transfer to a wire rack to cool completely.

Lemon and Almond Shortbread

⅔ cup superfine sugar

1 cup plus 2 tablespoons salted butter

1 medium egg yolk

2 cups all-purpose flour, sifted

1⅓ cups ground almonds

grated zest of 1 lemon

1 teaspoon lemon juice

Makes about 50 leaf cookies

Put all the ingredients into a food processor and mix until the cookie dough comes together or, alternatively, follow the method for the vanilla sablés (page 16). Wrap in plastic and chill for about 1 hour or up to 1 week.

When ready to bake, roll out the dough on a lightly floured work surface to about ⅛ inch thick. Using a sharp knife, cut out leaf shapes. (For other shapes, use templates or cookie cutters.) Place apart on several lightly buttered baking trays and cook in a preheated oven at 350°F for 12 to 15 minutes until just golden. Remove the cookies from the oven and cool on a wire rack.

The shortbread cookies can also be sandwiched together with jam or lemon curd, then served with tea or coffee, or as an accompaniment for desserts and ice-cream.

Chocolate Pepper Cookies

4 tablespoons salted butter, softened

6 tablespoons superfine sugar

4 tablespoons brown sugar

½ teaspoon vanilla extract

1 medium egg, beaten

¾ cup all-purpose flour, sifted

¼ cup unsweetened cocoa powder, sifted

1 teaspoon baking powder

1 teaspoon crushed black pepper

4 oz. unsweetened chocolate, finely chopped, or chocolate morsels

Makes 16 cookies

Using a wooden spoon or electric mixer, cream the butter with the superfine sugar, brown sugar, vanilla extract, and beaten egg. Add the sifted flour, sifted cocoa powder, baking powder, and the crushed black pepper. Stir in the chopped chocolate or chocolate pieces and, using your hands, bring the dough together.

Shape into a log about 2¾ inches diameter, wrap in plastic and chill for 1 hour or up to 1 week.

When ready to bake, cut the log into 16 slices. Roll each one into a ball, squash slightly, and place apart on several lightly buttered baking trays. Cook at 350°F for about 10 to 12 minutes. Remove from the oven and let cool on a wire rack.

two-tone cookies

Large quantities of these brown-and-white cookies are baked at Christmastime in Germany. They are made of two different colored doughs folded together to make various patterns. Choose two or three of these six designs—spiral, checkerboard and marble cookies are the simplest, the others slightly more complicated to assemble.

½ quantity vanilla sablé dough (page 16)

½ quantity chocolate sablé dough (page 16)

1 medium egg white

Makes 60 cookies

Make the vanilla and chocolate sablé doughs, wrap in plastic and chill for 1 hour. When ready to assemble, briefly knead the doughs separately to soften. Cut each one into portion sizes as instructed in the recipe for Spiral Cookies on this page, or the variations on pages 22 to 25. All should be baked as described below.

Spiral Cookies Roll out 4 oz. of vanilla dough on a lightly floured work surface into a rectangle 6½ x 5 inches. Roll 4 oz. of chocolate dough to the same size. Beat the egg white with 1 tablespoon water and brush over the rectangle of vanilla dough. Place the chocolate rectangle on top. Roll the double thickness to a rectangle 8 x 6½ inches. Trim the edges*. Brush the top with egg white mixture.

Starting from one of the long sides, roll up the dough into a log about 1¾-inches diameter. Wrap in plastic and chill for 1 hour. Alternatively, freeze the wrapped log for use at a later date, defrosting in the refrigerator overnight before using.

When ready to bake, slice the log into 20 rounds, ⅜ inch thick. Place apart on several lightly buttered baking trays and bake in a preheated oven at 400°F for 12 to 14 minutes, until golden. Remove from the oven and cool on a wire rack.

Checkerboard Repeat to the end of the first step* for Spiral Cookies.

1 Cut in half lengthwise into two strips. Brush one strip with the egg white and put the other on top.

2 Continue cutting and stacking the strips until there are 8 layers of chocolate and vanilla dough.

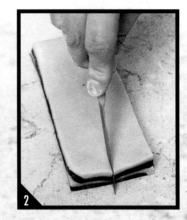

3 Using a small sharp knife, slice the layered dough lengthwise into 4 to 5 strips. If the dough becomes warm, chill for 30 minutes before continuing.

4 Brush one strip with egg white. Place the next strip on top, so a vanilla stripe appears on top of a chocolate one, giving a checkerboard effect. Repeat until all the strips are used. Trim the ends, wrap the log in plastic, and neaten its shape with the flat of your hand. Chill for about 1 hour. Slice into 20 squares ⅛ inch thick and bake as in the main recipe.

Spiral Combination Cookies

1 Make one two-tone spiral log (page 20,) and a checkerboard log (page 22.) Cut the checkerboard lengthwise into 5 strips, then place them side-by-side on the work surface to form a striped rectangle. Brush with egg white mixture.

2 Place the spiral log at the top end of the rectangle. Wrap the striped rectangle of dough around the log by rolling it slowly towards you, then roll it back-and-forth on the work surface into a log about 1¾ inches diameter. Trim the ends, wrap in plastic, and chill for 1 hour.

3 Slice into 40 rounds ⅜ inch thick and bake as in the main recipe (page 20.)

Bridget Riley Cookies An abstract inspired by the work of pop artist Bridget Riley. Make a Spiral Cookie log (page 20,) and cut it in half lengthwise.

Main picture Lay the halves, flat side down, on the work surface. Brush with water and twist together. Shape into a square log with the flat of your hand.

2 Trim the ends, wrap, and chill for 1 hour. Slice into 20 squares ⅜ inch thick and bake as in the main recipe (page 20.)

Butterflies Roll out 2½ oz. vanilla dough thinly to a square 4 x 4 inches. Roll out 4 oz. chocolate dough to the same size. Brush the egg white mixture over the vanilla square and put the chocolate square on top. Roll out to a larger square, 5½ x 5½ inches. Trim the edges. Cut it in half lengthwise, brush the strips with egg white mixture and stack one on top of the other. Repeat cutting and stacking once more, for an 8-layered log.

1 Using the side of your little finger, make deep channels down the length of the log on both sides. The log, in section, now resembles a figure 8.

2 Make two sausage shapes from 2½ oz. vanilla dough, and roll to the same length as the log. Insert the two pieces into the gaps on each side of the log and press into place. Gently shape it back into a log.

Main picture Roll out 2½ oz. vanilla dough into a rectangle 8 x 5 inches, brush with egg white and wrap around the log. Roll the log back-and-forth on the work surface to 1¾ inches diameter. Trim the ends, wrap in plastic and chill for 1 hour.

4 Slice the log into 20 rounds ⅜ inch thick and bake as in the main recipe (page 20.)

Catherine Wheels Take 1½ oz. of each dough and shape into 2 small logs. Roll out 3 oz. of each dough into 2 rectangles, 5½ x 4½ inches. Brush egg white mixture over the vanilla rectangle and top with the chocolate one. Roll to a square 5½ x 5½ inches, trim the edges and cut lengthwise into 7 strips.
1 Brush with water, then lay each strip lengthwise about halfway over the next one to create a stepped rectangle. Flatten slightly with your hand.
2 Put 2 logs, end-to-end, on top edge of rectangle, and wrap towards you.
Main picture Roll the whole log back-and-forth until the sides are smooth and the log is 1¼ inches diameter. Trim the ends, wrap, and chill for 1 hour.
4 Slice into 20 rounds ⅜ inch thick and bake as in the main recipe (page 20.)

Marble Cookies Use all the trimmings and any remaining bits of dough. Press them together and shape into a log. Wring the log slightly to give the inside a marbled effect. Wrap in plastic and chill for 1 hour. Slice the chilled log into rounds ⅜ inch thick and bake as in the main recipe (page 20.)

ginger cats

Miaow, miaow, who doesn't know a cat lover? Ideal as gifts, to decorate a cake, or for novelty place cards at a party. Don't worry about minor piping imperfections—it's part of the charm of baking.

I quantity stem ginger dough
(page 16)

To decorate:
2 oz. unsweetened chocolate
½ quantity lemon water
frosting (page 13)
red, yellow, and brown
food coloring
⅛ quantity royal icing, for
piping (page 12)
Makes 20 small cookies
or 10 large

Prepare the stem ginger dough, wrap in plastic, and chill for about 1 hour or up to 1 week.

Cut out cat templates (page 78) from a thin sheet of plastic or card, or draw templates freehand on paper first.

Briefly knead the chilled dough to soften. Roll out the dough on a lightly floured work surface to ¼ inch thick. Place the cat template on top and, using a small sharp knife, cut carefully around the edge. Place the cat shapes apart on several lightly buttered baking trays and cook in a preheated oven at 350°F for 13 to 15 minutes until golden. Remove from the oven and cool on a wire rack. When ready to decorate, use half the quantity of cookies for black cats and the rest for white or ginger cats.

To decorate Black Cats When the cookies have cooled completely, melt the chocolate (page 10) over a bowl of hot water or in a microwave. Brush the chocolate over the cookies, dabbing with the brush to resemble fur (page 8.) Let set for at least 1 hour before piping cat features.

To decorate White or Ginger Cats Brush the lemon water frosting evenly over the cookies and let set. For a tabby-cat appearance, while the frosting is still wet, dab on red, yellow, or brown coloring, or a mixture of colors. Let set for at least 1 hour before piping cat features.

Fill a paper piping bag with royal icing and use to outline the cat features on each cookie: pipe eyes, nose, mouth, whiskers, claws, and other markings. Let set for 1 hour.

Store the decorated cat cookies in an airtight container. Best eaten within 1 week, but will keep for up to 4 weeks.

To make Gingerbread Cats Use 1 quantity of gingerbread dough (page 19) instead of stem ginger dough and continue as before. When ready to bake, place the shapes apart on several baking trays lined with parchment paper and cook in a preheated oven at 350°F for 13 to 15 minutes. Remove from the oven and let cool on the baking trays for about 5 minutes, until firm enough to transfer to a wire rack to cool completely. Decorate and store as for ginger cats.

1

2

gingerbread santas and clowns

Jolly gingerbread cookies have become a trademark at Konditor & Cook, my pâtisserie shop in London. These colorful fellows are a little time-consuming to make, but for a children's party they are well worth the effort.

1 quantity gingerbread dough (page 19)   *Makes 14 gingerbread cookies*
1 quantity royal icing (page 12)
red food coloring

Briefly knead the chilled gingerbread dough to soften. Roll out the dough on a lightly floured work surface to about ⅛ inch thick.

Cut out santa shapes using a sharp knife and the template (page 78) or a traditional gingerbread cutter. To make the gingerbread hats, stick a small triangular piece of dough to each head. Gather all the trimmings and repeat rolling and cutting until all the dough is used. Place the gingerbread santas on several baking trays lined with parchment paper.

Bake in a preheated oven at 350°F for 13 to 15 minutes. Remove from the oven and let cool on the baking trays for 5 minutes, until firm enough to transfer to a wire rack to cool completely. If, after 5 minutes, the centers are still very soft, return to the oven for a further 5 minutes.

When ready to decorate, make several paper piping bags (page 8.) Fill 1 or 2 piping bags with half the royal icing and pipe all the white parts first; fur trimmings, facial features, and details such as coat fastenings.

1 First pipe the fur trimming and bobble of the hat, then the sleeves and around the jacket, followed by the trousers. Pipe 2 circles for the whites of the eyes. Pipe a big smile drawing the upper and lower lip in one flow—this will make their smiles look bigger.

Add red coloring to the remaining royal icing, and a few drops of water to make it a little softer. Transfer to a paper piping bag and cut off the tip.

2 Fill in the hat, jacket, and trousers with red icing, leaving a small space between the white and the red. Let dry for 1 hour. To personalize the santas, inscribe names in royal icing onto the frosted and dried cookies.

Wrap the cookies in cellophane bags and tie with ribbon or store in an airtight container. Best eaten within 1 week but will keep for up to 4 weeks.

To make Gingerbread Clowns (pages 30 to 31) follow the recipe for santas, letting them cool completely before decorating. Divide the royal icing in half. Leave one portion white to pipe the trimmings, then color the rest orange, red, green, yellow, and blue. Melt 2 oz. chocolate (page 10) ready to pipe the shoes (optional.) After piping each color, let dry for about 15 minutes before piping the next.

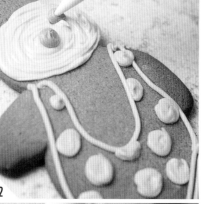

2

3

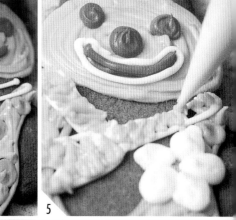

4

5

For the clowns

Decorate clowns in pairs.

Above Fill in the faces with pale orange royal icing, then pipe the costume outline, stripes and dots.

2 Add the red nose, eyes, and mouth.

3 Fill in the costume with green royal icing.

4 Pipe an outline of the necktie and gloves with white icing.

5 Outline the shape of the mouth with white royal icing and pipe a flower. Fill in the scarf with green and yellow stripes. Pipe yellow gloves and yellow center for the flower.

Below Style the hair with dark orange icing. Pipe the hat in blue and the border in green. Add white bobbles (page 8) to the hat.

Above Finally, pipe the clown's eyes and his brown shoes using melted chocolate.

christmas stars

Get your children to help make these baked Christmas tree decorations—it's enormous fun and adds a personal touch. Decorate the stars with dots, swirls, or names, or add festive messages in different languages. Wrap them in cellophane and attach to presents as unusual gift tags.

For inscribed stars the base should be large enough for the inscription. One cookie should weigh no more than about 1 oz.—if it is too heavy, the branches of the tree may not be able to bear the weight.

Briefly knead the chilled dough to soften. Roll out the dough on a lightly floured work surface to about ⅛ inch thick. Cut out stars using an 3-inch star-shaped cookie cutter or cut them out freehand using a sharp knife. Place apart on several baking trays lined with parchment paper. Using a skewer, make small holes in some cookies about ½ inch from the top edge. (The holes should be the same width as the ribbon.) Brush lightly with beaten egg and bake in a preheated oven at 350°F for 12 to 15 minutes, until just golden. Remove from the oven and cool on a wire rack.

To decorate the cookies, fill a paper piping bag with royal icing. Pipe swirls, dots and outlines, and while the royal icing is still wet press on the silver balls, if using. Let dry for at least 1 hour. Cut the ribbon into short lengths and tie through the holes in the cookies, ready to hang.

1 quantity vanilla sablé
  dough (page 16)

To decorate:
⅓ quantity royal icing
  (page 12)
1 medium egg, lightly beaten
20 inches ribbon, ¼ inch wide
½ oz. edible silver-coated
  sugar balls (optional)
Makes about 30 cookies

shortbread flowers

I am often asked to produce personalized cookies for weddings, birthdays, and corporate events. These flower-shaped cookies would be at home on any summery wedding table, at a garden-lover's birthday party, or at a *kaffeeklatsch* —a good gossip with friends over coffee and cookies.

1 quantity lemon and almond
   dough (page 19)
1 medium egg, lightly beaten

To decorate:
½ quantity lemon water
   frosting (page 13)
⅓ quantity royal icing
   (page 12)
yellow and orange food
   coloring
2 oz. unsweetened chocolate
½ oz. chocolate vermicelli
   (optional)
Makes about 30 cookies

Roll out the dough on a lightly floured work surface to about ⅛ inch thick. While the dough is still very cold and easy to work with, use a template (page 78) to cut out sunflower and lily shapes.

Roll out the trimmings and use a 3-inch fluted cookie cutter to cut out daisy shapes. Vary the size of the cutter if you have a complete set. Place the shapes apart on several baking trays lined with parchment paper. Put large shapes together on one sheet and small ones, such as the lilies, on another sheet so they will bake evenly.

Lightly brush the egg evenly over the surface of the cookies—avoid pools of egg or the cookies will become too dark. Bake in a preheated oven at 350°F for 12 to 15 minutes, until golden. The larger shapes will take a little longer to cook. Remove from the oven and cool the cookies on a wire rack.

Prepare the frostings, melt the chocolate (page 10) in a bowl over hot water or in a microwave. Use to decorate the cookies (pages 36 to 37.)

White Lilies **1** Lightly brush the cookies with lemon water frosting.

Main picture Outline the petals with royal icing and pipe a line in the center of each petal.

3 While the frosting is wet, arrange the stamens (page 8) in the center of each cookie and pipe dots of white icing for the flower parts.

Daisies Mark a small circle in the center, then pipe petals onto the cookies, using the crinkle edge as a guide. Try piping consecutive or alternate petals for another effect.

1 Starting at the center, lift the icing thread to the tip of the petal and return to the center. Repeat until all the petals are complete.

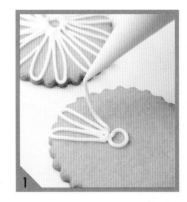

Below Daisy petals can also be filled in with more white royal icing. Fill the center of each flower with tiny dots or a circular blob of yellow royal icing.

To make Chrysanthemum Cookies, pipe only one side of the petal, from the center of the flower to the tip, stop piping and quickly drag the thread over the edge, leaving a neat pointed tip. Repeat for the other side of the petal.

Sunflowers Color one-third of the royal icing with a few drops of yellow. **1** Fill a paper piping bag with the yellow icing, mark the size of the seed head with a large circle, then pipe the petals. (While working, always cover any royal icing remaining in the bowl with a damp cloth to stop a crust forming.) Add a few drops of water to some of the yellow icing and use to fill in the petals. Let set for at least 1 hour.

2 To make a base for the sunflower seed head, pipe melted chocolate into the center of the flowers.

Main picture To make the seed head, pipe a grid of melted chocolate over the chocolate base. Alternatively, sprinkle with chocolate vermicelli. Let set for at least 1 hour.

happy sun cookies

From ancient times, the sun has been a powerful symbol. As well as making people smile, these Happy Sun Cookies taste good and could also double as a stunning centerpiece for a celebration cake.

½ quantity lemon and almond dough (page 19)

To decorate:
½ quantity lemon water frosting (page 13)
royal icing , made from 3½ oz. confectioner's sugar and 2 tablespoons egg white (page 12)
yellow, orange, and red food coloring
Makes about 14 cookies

Knead the chilled dough to soften. On a lightly floured surface, roll out to ⅛ inch thick and cut into rounds using a 4-inch cookie cutter. Gather the trimmings and continue rolling and cutting until all the dough has been used. Using a large 1-inch piping nozzle or small cookie cutter, cut scallops around the edge of each cookie to make the sun's rays. For a pointed corona, make triangular cuts around the edge.

Place the shapes apart on several lightly buttered baking trays and cook in a preheated oven at 350°F for 12 to 15 minutes, until just golden. Remove from the oven and let cool on a wire rack.

Add a few drops of yellow food coloring to the lemon water frosting. Put a few drops of orange or red coloring on a small plate or saucer. Prepare the royal icing and divide among 3 small bowls; color one pink, one yellow, and one orange.

1 Brush the cookies with yellow water frosting. Dip a second brush into the orange or red coloring and dab around the edge or over half the face of the sun. This will give a 3-dimensional appearance. Let dry for 1 hour.

2 Use 2 colors of royal icing to pipe the suns' rays. Pipe features too, if you wish, giving them a big happy smile. Alternate the colors of rays and suns. My favorite is a yellow face with orange rays overlaid with pink piping.

1

2

hallowe'en cookies

Hallowe'en is a traditional American festival, but it is also widely celebrated in other parts of the world. Devils, ghosts, and of course pumpkins are all symbols associated with Hallowe'en. These spooky cookies are made with crushed black pepper, which enhances the chocolate flavor while firing up the taste buds.

1 quantity chocolate pepper
  dough (page 19)

To decorate:
⅓ quantity royal icing
  (page 12)
2 tablespoons confectioner's
  sugar
orange, green, and red
  food coloring
Makes 16 cookies

Make the Chocolate Pepper Cookies (page 19,) then let cool completely on a wire rack before decorating.

To decorate Ghost Cookies To make a stencil, draw the outline of the cookie on a piece of thin card, then draw the ghost shape from the template (page 78) to fit within the circle. Cut out the stencil using a sharp blade. Cut 2 small disks of card for the eyes.

Place the stencil on a cookie and, using a pair of tweezers, position the eyes. Dust confectioner's sugar over the top.

Using tweezers, carefully lift off the eye-disks, then the stencil, to reveal a ghost. Shake the icing sugar off the card before dusting another 3 cookies.

Color 1 tablespoon of royal icing green, and divide the rest in half. Color one half orange and the other red.

To decorate Pumpkin Cookies Fill a paper piping bag with orange icing and pipe an outline onto 6 cookies adding eyes, nose, and a jagged mouth. Fill in the gaps with orange icing. Using the cracked lines of the cookies as a guide, pipe lines for a distressed effect. To finish, pipe a dot of green icing on the pumpkin's head. Let set for at least 1 hour.

To decorate Devil Cookies Fill a paper piping bag with red icing and pipe an outline of the face, large pointed ears, and horns. Pipe long triangular-shaped eyes, a nose, and a sharp evil grin, then fill in the face. Pipe the devil's tail and a three-pronged fork. Finish by piping distressed lines as before. Let set for at least 1 hour.

Variation: The Ghost Cookies may also be decorated with royal icing. Leave some of the icing white and use to pipe the outline of a hood, flowing sleeves, legs and facial features. Fill in the gaps with icing. Let set for at least 1 hour.

decorating cakes

Modern graphics and creative use of color have always been my inspiration for cake design. Many kinds of art can be a great source of ideas—think of prints, fabrics or wallpapers, look at pop culture, modern graphics, or graffiti.

Don't worry if your designs include a few imperfections—choose a style that allows you to make a few minor mistakes—then make them part of the overall design.

Above all, your cakes should taste absolutely delicious. I always begin with a traditional cake base with wonderful flavor, before I even think about decorating it. So remember—food must give pleasure to your taste buds as well as your eyes.

lemon victoria sponge

Victoria sponge is a flexible recipe that can be flavored in many ways. Try adding other citrus fruit, or capture the aromas of an Italian coffee bar with espresso and a hint of cinnamon.

¾ cup plus 2 tablespoons salted butter, softened, plus extra for greasing
grated zest of 2 lemons
a pinch of salt
1 cup superfine sugar
4 medium eggs, beaten
1⅛ cups self-rising flour, sifted

To decorate:
2 tablespoons unsweetened cocoa powder or confectioner's sugar
Makes one 10-inch round cake

Grease a 10-inch round cake pan and line with parchment paper. Grease again and dust with flour.

Using a wooden spoon or electric mixer, cream the butter with the lemon zest and salt until creamy. (Mixing the lemon zest with the butter intensifies the flavors.) Add the sugar and beat vigorously until the mixture is light and fluffy.

Add the beaten eggs, 1 tablespoon at a time, beating well after each addition. If necessary, mix in 1 to 2 tablespoons of flour to prevent the mixture curdling.

Using a large metal spoon, gently fold in the flour in 3 batches. Spoon the cake mixture into the prepared cake pan and spread evenly.

Level the surface with a palette knife then bake on the middle rack of a preheated oven at 350°F for about 25 to 30 minutes. The center is cooked when the surface of the sponge springs back when lightly pressed. To double check, insert a skewer or a small knife into the center of the sponge. If it comes out clean (or with a few tiny crumbs attached,) the sponge is cooked: if a little raw cake mixture sticks to the skewer or knife, bake for 5 to 10 minutes more.

Remove from the oven and cool in the pan on a wire rack. After about 30 minutes the sponge can be turned out of the cake pan. Let cool completely before cutting and filling.

If required, the sponge can then be sliced into 3 layers, wrapped in plastic, and frozen for later use. When ready to decorate, defrost overnight.

To decorate, place a stencil over the cake and dust with unsweetened cocoa powder or confectioner's sugar. Lift off the stencil and serve.

To make a Victoria Sponge Layer Cake, grease and line two 7-inch sandwich pans. Bake in a preheated oven at 350°F for about 20 to 25 minutes. Test by pressing or piercing as in the main recipe, then let cool as before. Fill and cover with the filling or frosting of your choice.

orange genoese sponge

The Genoese is the airiest and lightest of sponges and even better with a filling of lightly whipped cream, or a sprinkling of liqueur or syrup. Sugar frosted fruits give a bright, fresh effect, adding a touch of elegance.

Base-line a 10–inch round cake pan or springform pan with parchment paper. Grease with butter and dust with flour.

Put the egg whites and salt in a large bowl. (To clean the bowl thoroughly, wipe with a little lemon juice or vinegar, rinse with cold water, and dry with a clean cloth.) Using an electric hand-mixer, begin beating at a slow speed to break up the egg whites. Switch to a higher setting, then add 2 tablespoons of sugar. Continue beating and adding sugar until two-thirds of the sugar has been used. At this stage the egg whites should have good volume and hold stiff peaks.

Add the remaining sugar, the egg yolks and orange zest. Using a large metal spoon, gently fold in the flour and baking powder in 3 batches, moving the spoon through the middle to combine any pockets of flour that remain unmixed.

Slowly pour the butter over the surface of the mixture and gently fold in, cutting through the mixture with a large metal spoon to retain as much air as possible. Spoon the sponge mixture into the prepared cake pan. Bake on the middle rack of a preheated oven at 350°F for about 25 minutes. The center is cooked if the surface springs back when lightly pressed. To double check, insert a skewer or a small knife into the center—the cake is cooked when it comes out clean (or with a few tiny crumbs attached)—if a little of the raw cake mixture sticks to the skewer or knife, bake for a further 5 to 10 minutes.

Remove from the oven, let cool in the pan and turn out when cold. (If required, it can be sliced into 3 layers, wrapped in plastic and frozen for later use. Defrost overnight.)

Cut the sponge carefully into 3 layers. Lightly whip the cream until soft peaks form. Divide three-quarters of the cream between the layers, then spoon the remaining cream in a circle around the top edge of the cake. To frost the fruit, brush with egg white then dip in sugar. Transfer to a wire rack to dry for at least 1 hour.

To decorate, arrange the frosted fruit over the whipped cream, around the edge of the cake.

6 medium eggs, separated
a pinch of salt
¾ cup superfine sugar
grated zest of 2 oranges
1 cup all-purpose flour, sifted, plus extra for dusting
1 teaspoon baking powder
6 tablespoons salted butter, melted and cooled

To decorate:
1¾ cups light whipping cream
red currants, kumquats, and cape gooseberries (physallis)
1 medium egg white, lightly beaten
sugar, to coat
Makes one 10-inch layer-cake

carrot cake

Carrot cake recipes vary—many are made with vegetable oil and wholemeal flour and claim to be healthy. This one is different in that it contains very little flour and no fat. Toasted hazelnuts and a moist texture make it similar to a traditional Swiss recipe. For a decorated version, see page 60, where the carrots are given a fun treatment.

5 medium eggs, separated
a pinch of salt
1 cup superfine sugar
8 oz. carrots, grated
grated zest of 1 lemon
juice of ½ lemon
⅓ cup all-purpose flour, sifted
1 teaspoon baking powder
1¾ cups hazelnuts, lightly
   toasted and ground
½ teaspoon ground cinnamon

To decorate:
3½ oz. apricot jam, warmed
½ quantity lemon water
   frosting (page 13)
⅓ cup hazelnuts, toasted
Makes one 10-inch cake

Grease a 10-inch round cake pan and line the base and sides with parchment paper. Put the egg whites and salt in a large bowl. Using an electric hand-mixer, begin beating, then gradually add the sugar, 2 tablespoons at a time, increasing the addition of sugar as the meringue begins to firm up and increase in volume. (At this stage the meringue should be creamy and hold soft peaks.) Add the egg yolks and beat for a few seconds.

Mix the carrots, lemon zest, and juice in a bowl. Mix the flour, baking powder, ground hazelnuts, and cinnamon in a second bowl. Using a large metal spoon, gently fold the carrots and the flour mixture alternately into the meringue. The consistency should be very wet and runny.

Pour the mixture into the prepared cake pan. Bake on the middle rack of a preheated oven at 350°F for about 25 to 30 minutes, or until the cake springs back when lightly pressed or when a skewer inserted in the center comes out clean.

Remove from the oven and cool on a wire rack. Refrigerate overnight for easy handling. Brush with the jam, spread the top with frosting and decorate with hazelnuts.

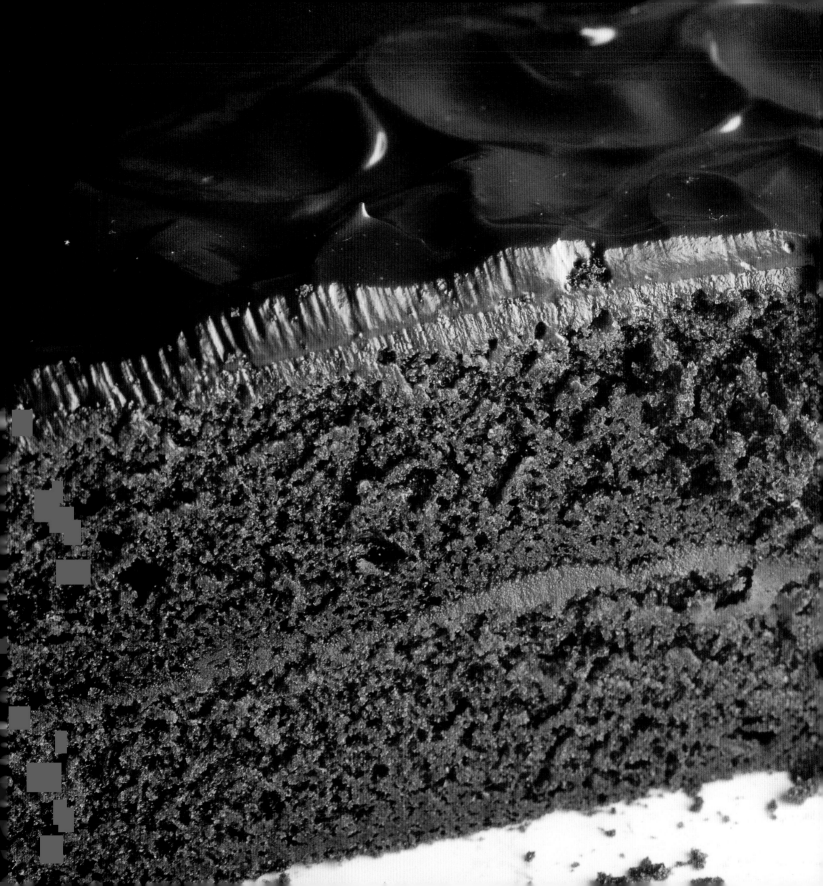

dark chocolate sponge

This ultimate chocolate cake is a taste bud treat for all chocoholics. With a texture so smooth and a taste so rich, a little goes a long way. Use the sponge recipe to make the base for a wedding cake or a chocolate spectacular, such as the Konditor Cone (page 72).

Grease two 7-inch sandwich pans and line the bases with parchment paper. Melt the chocolate in a saucepan with half the milk and half the sugar. Stir the mixture constantly to prevent the chocolate sticking to the bottom of the saucepan. Remove the pan from the heat and let cool.

Using a wooden spoon or electric mixer, cream the butter with the remaining sugar. Beat in the eggs, a little at a time, until light and fluffy. If necessary, add 1 to 2 tablespoons of flour to the mixture when beating in the eggs to prevent curdling.

Sift the flour, baking powder, and cocoa powder together. Using a large metal spoon, gently fold the flour mixture into the creamed mixture in 3 batches.

While the chocolate is still warm, fold it into the cake mixture. Stir in the remaining milk to form a runny consistency, then divide the mixture between the two prepared sandwich pans.

Bake on the middle rack of a preheated oven at 325°F for about 20 to 25 minutes, or until the sponge springs back when lightly pressed or when a skewer inserted in the center comes out clean. Remove the cake from the oven and let cool in the pans. Sandwich together with the ganache, then cover with more ganache.

3½ oz. unsweetened chocolate, chopped

1 cup milk

1⅓ cups brown sugar

2 medium eggs, beaten

7 tablespoons salted butter, softened

1 cup plus 1 tablespoon all-purpose flour

1 teaspoon baking powder

2 tablespoons unsweetened cocoa powder

To decorate:

1 quantity chocolate ganache (page 10)

Makes one 7-inch layer-cake

golden simnel fruitcake

This traditional Easter Simnel Cake was named for Lambert Simnel, the son of an Oxford baker, who was a pretender to the English throne after the Wars of the Roses. Pardoned by the King, Henry VII, Simnel later worked as a baker in the Royal household and made this special crown-shaped cake in honor of the King.

1 orange

1 lemon

¾ cup salted butter, softened

a pinch of ground nutmeg

a pinch of ground cloves

¼ teaspoon salt

1 cup golden raisins

1½ cups dried currants

1 cup glacé cherries, chopped

1 cup mixed candied peel

3 tablespoons brandy

⅔ cup superfine sugar

2 tablespoons milk

4 medium eggs, beaten

1⅔ cups all-purpose flour

1 teaspoon baking powder

1 quantity homemade
    almond paste (page 10)

1 medium egg yolk

Makes one 8-inch cake

This cake requires forward planning. The day before baking, grate the orange zest and lemon zest into a small bowl. Mix in the nutmeg, cloves, salt and ⅔ cup of the butter. Cover and leave at room temperature overnight, to develop the flavors. Put the raisins, currants, cherries and mixed peel in a large bowl. Mix the brandy, orange and lemon juices and pour over the fruits. Stir well, cover and leave overnight.

To bake, use the remaining butter to grease an 8-inch round cake pan, then line the base and sides with a double layer of parchment paper.

With a wooden spoon or electric hand-mixer, cream the butter-spice mixture (if necessary, soften in a bowl set over hot water) with the sugar and milk until light and fluffy. Sift the flour and baking powder into a bowl. Beat a quarter of the eggs into the creamed butter-spice mixture, then beat in 1 to 2 tablespoons flour. Repeat until all the eggs have been added, then fold in the remaining flour and the soaked fruit. Spoon half the mixture into the prepared cake pan.

Roll one-third of the almond paste between 2 sheets of thick plastic, to a thin round slightly smaller than the pan. Put the round of almond paste on top of the mixture in the pan and cover with the remaining cake mixture. Level the top and bake on the middle rack of a preheated oven at 300°F for 2 hours. Put a water-filled ovenproof bowl on the bottom rack of the oven, so the cake will stay moist.

After 1 hour check the cake. Cover with parchment paper if it is dark on top, yet still uncooked in the center. Test again after 30 minutes (page 44.) When cooked, remove from the oven, let cool in the pan, then turn it out but leave wrapped. Wrap well in foil and store for 2 weeks to let the cake mature.

To decorate, roll out one-third of the almond paste between 2 sheets of thick plastic to a thin round. Place on top of the cake and pinch the edge to crimp. With the remaining almond paste, roll out 11 small balls and put in a circle around the edge of the cake. Brush with egg yolk and brown the almond paste under a preheated broiler, until golden.

pop cake

Cake decorating is fun if you choose bold and colorful designs. For a large name or number use freehand graffiti-style writing—it's not difficult and any irregularities become part of the overall design.

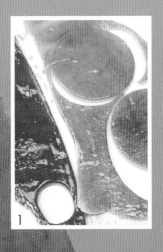

Make the decorations first so they can dry overnight. Roll 3½ oz. marzipan between 2 sheets of plastic to ¹⁄₁₆-inch thick. Cut into 3 unequally sized strips. Brush one with yellow coloring, one red, and one orange. Brush with jam and let dry overnight.

1 Cut circles with various sized cookie cutters (dip them in cold water to stop sticking). Cut some in half for the edges. Transfer to parchment paper and set aside

Spoon the sponge mixture into an 8-inch square cake pan, greased and base-lined. Bake in a preheated oven at 350°F for 25 to 30 minutes. Remove, cool, then slice into 3 layers, fill with two-thirds of the lemon chiffon frosting, and spread the rest over the top. Roll 7 oz. marzipan between 2 sheets of plastic to fit the top of the cake. Transfer the marzipan to the cake (trim the excess later.) Flood the surface with lemon water frosting. Let set for 1 hour. Trim the edges with a sharp, wet knife.

Mix confectioner's sugar with egg white and reserve 1 tablespoon of mixture. Color the rest in orange, purple, and yellow. For large bold lettering, pipe an orange outline.

2 Fill in with purple frosting and highlight in yellow. To give the marzipan shapes a raised effect, pipe the reserved frosting onto the back of each. Transfer to the cake.

3 Put large shapes next to small shapes in different colors to achieve wild effects.

1 quantity lemon victoria
    sponge mixture (page 44)

To decorate:
½ quantity lemon chiffon
    frosting (page 10)
7 oz. marzipan
½ quantity lemon water
    frosting, made to a thick
    consistency (page 13)

Marzipan decorations:
3½ oz. marzipan
yellow, red, orange, and
    purple food coloring,
2½ oz. apricot jam, warmed
5 tablespoons
    confectioner's sugar
1 tablespoon egg white
Makes one 8-inch
square cake

magic cakes

These cakes work colorful magic—customize them with animal motifs for a children's party and see all the faces light up. For a grown-up version decorate with appropriate designs and symbols and add a few witty slogans. Jumble in one big happy mosaic and see the magic work!

1 quantity lemon victoria
    sponge mixture (page 44)
juice of 2 lemons
4 tablespoons apricot jam,
    warmed and sieved
8 oz. marzipan
4 quantities (2 lb.) fondant
    frosting (page 13)

To decorate:
⅓ quantity royal icing
    (page 12)
food colorings
2 oz. unsweetened chocolate,
    melted
glacé cherries
cocoa powder
colored dragées

Makes 28 small cakes

Put the lemon victoria sponge mixture into a greased and base-lined baking tray, 8¼ x 12 x 1 inch. Bake in a preheated oven at 350°F for 20 to 25 minutes as described on page 44. Remove from the oven, let cool for 30 minutes in the tray, then turn out onto a wire rack to cool completely. Brush the top of the cake with half the lemon juice (this makes the flavor sharp and compensates for the sweet sugar coating.) Apply a thin layer of jam with a palette knife.

Roll out the marzipan between 2 sheets of thick plastic to the same size as the cake. Carefully transfer the marzipan to the cake and gently smooth the top with your hand. Chill for about 1 hour.

Using a ruler or straightedge, measure the marzipan-covered cake into 28 squares, each 1¾ x 1¾ inches. Mark the marzipan with indentations to make cutting easier. Cut the cake into squares using a serrated knife following the indentations as a guide. (Dip the knife blade into cold water to stop the

marzipan from dragging or sticking.) Keep the squares of cake together and brush the tops with a thin layer of the warmed, sieved jam. Warm the fondant frosting (page 13) with the remaining lemon juice to 130°F.

Divide the fondant frosting between 4 small bowls. Leave one portion white and color the other 3 in yellow, red, and orange respectively. Alternatively, add your own choice of colors, from pale pastels to bold primary colors.

Separate the squares of cake and carefully dip each one into the prepared fondant frosting of your choice. Transfer to a wire rack set over a tray or baking parchment and let dry for at least 20 minutes.

When dry, lift the cakes off the rack with a small palette knife and place in white paper cases. Decorate them in your choice of the designs, shown opposite and overleaf, then package them in a pretty box or decorative plate.

Ladybird Cut a glacé cherry in half, then pipe a dot of royal icing into the cut side. Gently press the cherry, cut side down, onto one of the cakes.

1 Using a paper piping bag filled with melted chocolate, pipe a head and a line down the middle of the cherry.

2 Pipe spots and 3 legs on either side of the line.

Bumble Bee 1 Pipe 4 yellow stripes onto a magic cake, then pipe alternate chocolate stripes between the yellow ones. Pipe large round eyes using melted chocolate.

2 Using white royal icing, pipe outlines of wings onto the body, then fill in.

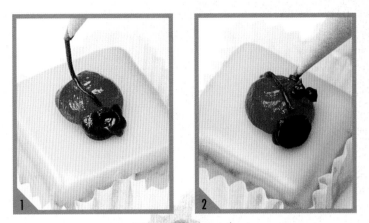

Forget-me-nots 1 Using pale blue royal icing, pipe tiny four- and five-petalled flowers onto magic cakes.

2 Using yellow icing, pipe tiny dots onto the centers of the flowers.

Below Finally, pipe green dots at random over each cake.

Cat 1 Color a little marzipan with unsweetened cocoa. Make a tiny chocolate ball and flatten slightly. Make indentations for eyes and ears. Pipe white eyes and whiskers then add a chocolate nose and chocolate dots on the eyes.

Elephant 2 Form a small piece of marzipan into a tapered shape and bend it up to make a trunk (page 9.) Make small indentations for the eyes and the wrinkles on the trunk. Add large ears in a contrasting color. Pipe on eyes and eyebrows.

Frog 1 Place a small dot of green royal icing in the middle of a cake and pipe frog's legs at the base.

2 Stick a dragée onto the dot. Pipe 2 green eyes.

3 Pipe a white dot onto each eye, then pipe a chocolate dot onto the white for contrast.

4 Pipe a wide mouth with red icing.

Sheep 1 Using white royal icing, pipe a fluffy, woolly white sheep's body onto the cake.

2 Pipe a head and legs using melted chocolate.

coiffured carrot cakes

With their fresh green leaves clipped and curled, these fancy cakes are a jolly addition to any child's birthday party. The best thing is they're colorful and fun to make.

Make and bake the carrot cake in a greased and base-lined baking tray, 12 x 8¼ x 1 inch, as described on page 48. Remove from the oven, cool in the tray, then turn out the cake upside down onto a large board so the base of the cake becomes the top. Pour the lemon water frosting evenly over the top of the cake. Using a palette knife, spread the frosting into the corners. Let dry and set for about 1 hour.

To prepare the carrots, color the marzipan with a few drops of orange coloring, then roll it into a log and slice into 20 pieces. Cover with plastic wrap.

1 To shape the carrots, roll each piece of marzipan into a round smooth ball, then mold each to a carrot shape with your fingers. Using a special marzipan tool, round-bladed knife, or wooden skewer make indentations for the eyes. To make their smiles use a marzipan tool or the edge of a round piping nozzle. Reserve a little white royal icing for the eyes, then in separate bowls color the rest in different shades of green for the hair, starting with plain green, then adding a touch of yellow or blue coloring.

2 Place the frosted cake on a board. Trim the edges with a sharp knife, then cut into 20 pieces, 2 x 2½ inches. Top with the marzipan carrots and pipe white icing into the eyes. Pipe chocolate dots onto the eyes so each pair looks in the same direction.

3 Pipe wavy lines or other shapes of green icing to make the leafy hair.

1 quantity carrot cake
    mixture (page 48)
1 quantity lemon water
    frosting (page 13)

To decorate:
3½ oz. marzipan
orange, green, yellow, and
    blue food coloring
royal icing, made with
    2½ cups confectioner's
    sugar (page 12)
1 oz. unsweetened chocolate,
    melted
Makes 20 small cakes

chocolate velvet cake

The irregular folds of this cake covering are dusted with cocoa powder to create a soft, velvety appearance. For the base, bake your favorite chocolate cake or use the Dark Chocolate Sponge (page 50.)

2 quantities dark chocolate sponge mixture (page 50)
1 quantity chocolate ganache (page 10)
1 oz. unsweetened cocoa
2 oz. unsweetened chocolate, melted

Whiskey Syrup:
3 tablespoons sugar
½ cup orange juice
grated zest of 1 orange
¼ cup whiskey

Covering:
1 tablespoon glucose (from drugstores) or whiskey
1 lb. marzipan
2 oz. unsweetened cocoa powder, sifted
Makes one 10-inch cake

To make the whiskey syrup, put the sugar and ⅓ cup water in a saucepan and bring to the boil. Remove from the heat, add the orange juice and zest, let cool, then add the whiskey.

To make the covering, knead the glucose or whiskey into the marzipan, add the cocoa powder and mix thoroughly. Chill until needed.

Make the chocolate sponges in two 10-inch round cake pans and bake for 25 to 30 minutes as described on page 50. Cool, then cut one of the sponges into 2 layers, one thicker than the other (the thick layer will form the base, the thin layer the lid.) Cut the second sponge into 1½-inch cubes.

Soak the cubes in a bowl with three-quarters of the whiskey syrup. Mix in three-quarters of the ganache (don't break up the cubes too much.) Stick the sponge base onto a cake board with a little ganache and brush with whiskey syrup. Scoop the soaked cubes on top and pat into a dome shape. Put the sponge lid on top. Brush with the remaining whiskey syrup, cover with plastic, and smooth with your hands to

form a neat dome shape. Chill for 1 hour. Remove the plastic and brush with the remaining ganache. Roll the chocolate marzipan covering between 2 thick plastic sheets to a 16-inch circle, ¹⁄₁₆-inch thick. Place on a flat metal tray.

1 Mold the marzipan for a wavy effect, then slide it off the tray and onto the cake. Carefully adjust the waves for extra drama. The larger you make the waves, the groovier and more sculptured the finished cake will look.

2 Trim excess marzipan from around the base.

3 Place the cake, still on its board, on a large sheet of paper and dust generously with cocoa powder. (Move the cake as you dust, so the cocoa can collect between the folds.) Carefully shake off the excess by holding the cake sideways and tapping it gently underneath. Place on a flat serving dish, then pipe a frilly border of melted chocolate.

Variation: To flavor the sponge with a hint of orange, use Cointreau syrup instead of whiskey syrup.

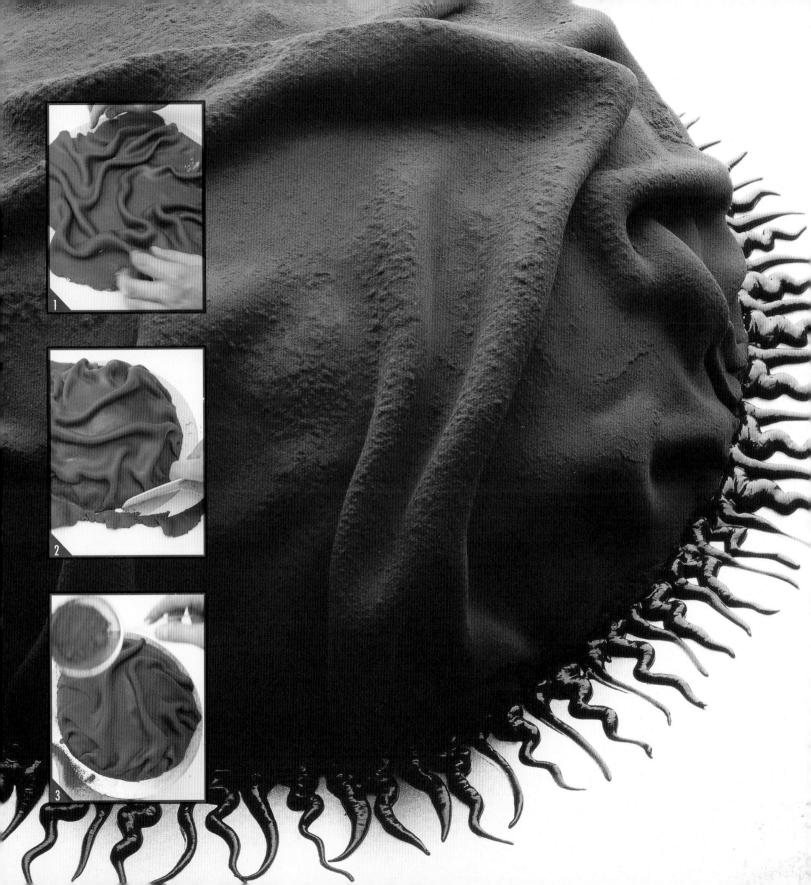

chocolate celebration cake

This orange-flavored sponge cake is richly decorated with structural shapes piped from three kinds of chocolate; plain, milk, and white. Some of the shapes are raised to create a three-dimensional effect, so the tactile surface and the resulting shadows create interesting surfaces on the cake. The decorations for this unusual cake are inspired by the Milky Way and the stars, moon, sun, and planets.

Make and bake the sponge in a greased and base-lined 10-inch round cake pan, as described on page 46. Remove from the oven, cool in the pan, then turn out onto a board. Using a large serrated knife, cut the cake into 3 layers. Spread two-thirds of the chocolate butter frosting onto 2 of the layers. Sandwich the filled layers together, then cover the top and sides of the cake with the remaining frosting. Chill for 1 hour.

Cover the cake with half the chocolate ganache and chill for 1 hour, or until set. Coat the cake with a second layer of ganache, reheating it first if necessary. Level the surface with a palette knife. Chill for at least 1 hour, or until set.

Meanwhile, prepare several paper piping bags (page 8) and melt the 3 kinds of chocolate in 3 separate cups over a small saucepan of hot water, or in a microwave (page 10.) Pipe the chocolate star, moon, planet, and sun decorations (page 66) and use to decorate the covered cake (page 67).

1 quantity orange genoese
 sponge mixture (page 46)
½ quantity quick butter
 frosting with chocolate
 (page 10)
1 quantity chocolate ganache
 (page 10)

To decorate:
2 oz. unsweetened chocolate
2 oz. milk chocolate
2 oz. white chocolate
extra quantities of
 unsweetened, milk, and
 white chocolate, for the
 chocolate mounts
Makes one 10-inch cake

Main picture On a sheet of parchment
paper, pipe the outlines for the white chocolate
stars and the moons, then fill in with white chocolate.

2 Pipe milk chocolate designs, such as the stars and Saturn rings.

3 and 4 Add contrasting squiggles in plain chocolate. Let dry.

5 and 6 Pipe simple swirls and dots in a wavy pattern directly onto the
cake, extending it occasionally down the sides for extra drama.

5

6

To attach the shapes, dab a little melted chocolate onto small set pieces of chocolate and stick them onto the cake. This will provide a mounting block for the shapes. Carefully lift the chocolate shapes off the parchment paper with the tip of a small knife and secure onto the mounts with more of the melted chocolate.

Main picture Pipe dots of white chocolate.

golden celebration cake

For a grand event such as a wedding or special anniversary, this cake is worth a little extra effort. The base recipe is the Golden Simnel Fruitcake, without the almond paste filling and topping (page 52) and it can be baked two weeks ahead to allow it to mature. Add extra sparkle with an elegant 23½ carat gold leaf decoration: gold leaf is expensive but no other gold coloring can match the luster of the real thing. Stick the gold leaf onto thinly rolled sheets of marzipan and use them as cladding, or as a base to cut your ornaments.

Remove the cooked fruit cake from its wrapping and brush the top and sides with the apricot jam. Roll two-thirds of the almond paste into a sheet about ¼-inch thick, large enough to cover the entire cake. Drape the almond paste over the cake, level the top and sides, then trim any excess from the base. Flatten the sides with a plastic scraper to achieve a more defined edge at the top.

To make the heart decoration, set aside a walnut-sized piece from the remaining almond paste.

Secure the cake to a cake board or plate with a little royal icing. Two coatings of royal icing are necessary for a perfect finish. First put a large quantity of the icing on top of the cake. Using a palette knife, spread it over the top and around the sides, rotating the cake board or plate at the same time. With the tip of the palette knife, smooth the icing around the sides for an even finish.

Run a straight-edged scraper around the sides of the cake. (Do this in one fluid movement to avoid any steps in the icing.) Straighten the edges and level the top with the palette knife, moving it from edge to edge and lifting it as you go over the middle. Scrape any excess icing back in the bowl. Turn the cake slightly and repeat until the entire edge is sharp and defined. Set aside to dry for 4 hours.

Apply a second layer of royal icing. Pat around the edge with a palette knife, lifting slightly to create a frilly edge. Let dry for about 1 hour, then decorate (pages 70 to 71).

1 golden fruitcake (page 52)

To decorate:
2½ oz. apricot jam, warmed
1 quantity homemade
   almond paste (page 10)
1 quantity royal icing
   (page 12)
6 sheets edible 23½ carat
   gold leaf (available from
   specialist sugarcraft shops)
red food coloring
Makes one 8-inch
round cake

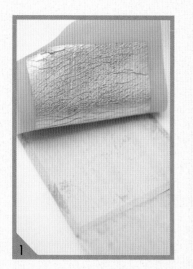

To make the gold decoration, roll the remaining almond paste thinly
between 2 thick sheets of plastic. Cut the paste into 5 equal squares.

1 Place each almond paste square on a sheet of gold leaf. Lift off at once
and trim the excess almond paste. Roll the trimmings and use to
cover the last sheet of gold leaf. Let dry overnight on
parchment paper.

2 Cut 4 gold leaf panels in half lengthwise to make 8.
Pipe a little royal icing onto the back of each
panel and press them onto the side of the cake.

3 Fill a paper piping bag with fresh icing and pipe
the connecting lines—the effect is like leather stitching
or the spine of a ring binder.

Main picture Cut another gold leaf panel into triangular rays of
gold, making 4 long, 4 medium, and 8 short or straight, with one
oblique end, rather than triangular. To make the gold buttons, using a
1-inch piping nozzle, cut out 8 disks from the remaining gold panel.

5 Pipe royal icing on the back of the rays, making it thicker at the sharp end. This lifts them, leaving a shadow gap, so the design appears lighter.

6 Mix red coloring into the reserved ball of almond paste. Mold into a heart shape or flatten and cut with a heart-shaped cutter. Dab a little icing onto the back of the heart and press it onto the center of the cake.

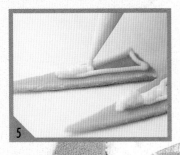

Main picture Arrange the gold rays around the heart so they stand away from the surface of the cake. Attach the gold buttons and pipe decorative edges to finish.

To make a Glittering Christmas cake, cut the almond paste and gold leaf squares into stars, trees, or angels. Decorate the cake with silver balls, almond dragées, or chocolates. Instead of the gold leaf border, use a wired gold ribbon and tie it in a bow on one side of the cake.

konditor cone

The Konditor Cone has become my signature cake—a very modern and stylish centerpiece adorned with iced ornaments and sheer ribbon that suits any important celebration. It is blend of a French *croquembouche* and an English wedding cake, and I was inspired to make my first cone by two events; a friend wanted an unusual, unconventional cake—and a short scene in the film *Cyrano de Bergerac*, showing oversized cakes, opulent pies, and meringues.

For the iced ornaments use the templates on page 79 or draw your own. Begin with simple designs such as hearts, flowers, stars, and crescent moons, then, when you feel more confident of your piping skills, choose more complex shapes, such as these more bizarre forms found on a coral reef.

3 quantities dark chocolate sponge mixture (page 50)
1½ quantities chocolate ganache (page 10)
2 lb. marzipan
1 quantity royal icing, and set aside 5½ oz. royal icing
 without glycerine, to make the ornaments
 8 feet of ribbon, 2 inches wide
Makes 1 cake (45 servings),
10 inches diameter, 16 inches tall

This cake is perfect for a modern-day feast or celebration such as a wedding, a special anniversary, or a birthday, and it can be designed to fit a specific occasion. Depending on the style you want, decide on a theme and make decorative royal icing ornaments appropriate to the celebration. Nautical, flower, star, and moon themes are simple to make, but relevant motifs can be tailor-made to suit the event and the guests of honor depending, of course, on your piping skill. The choice of ribbon changes the appearance dramatically—gold always looks festive, special and smart, while pastel organza is more romantic. For a contemporary twist, use fresh-colored gingham or blue and gold wired ribbon. Other colorful ribbons can also be used to great effect.

Prepare the sponge and divide the mixture among 4 cake pans (two of 10 inches and two 8 inches), or bake the sponge mixture in one large tray, 16 x 13 x 1 inches, then cut to the required sizes.

1 Use a conical pan or mold, stand it upside down in a large container (such as a champagne bucket), then line the inside of the cone with parchment paper.

2 Using a small serrated knife, cut pieces from the sponge to fit inside the cone mold.

3 Place the smallest sponge inside the conical mold. Add some chocolate ganache then place the next, slightly larger sponge in the cone.

4 Continue adding layers of sponge pieces (if the sponge layers are too small use extra sponge trimmings to fill the gaps) and spread each layer with more ganache.

5 The last layer should be in one piece, as this will form the base of the cake. Put the container, cone mold, and cake in the refrigerator, cover, and leave to set overnight.

6 Turn out the cake onto a plate and carefully remove the parchment paper from the side of the cake. Cover with a thin layer of ganache. For a perfect tip, shape a piece of marzipan into a miniature cone and stick on top.

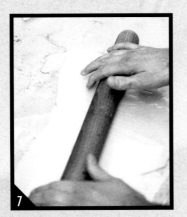

7 Roll out the remaining marzipan between 2 sheets of thick plastic to about ¼ inch thick.

8 Ideally the marzipan should be in one piece, but it can be done in sections if they are well pieced together. It will help to make a template of the cone.

9 Cover the cake with the marzipan and trim excess from the base.

10 Smooth the surface with plastic.

11 Apply the first layer of royal icing (with glycerine) with a palette knife, smoothing it well.

12 Pull a strip of parchment paper upwards over the icing to smooth further. Let dry for at least 4 hours before applying the next layer.

13 Before applying the final layer of royal icing, transfer the cake to a thick cake board or plate. Apply the final layer and smooth as before. Fill several small paper piping bags with the royal icing set aside for the ornaments. Pipe loops (to take the ribbon) onto sheets of parchment.

14 Use the templates or pipe shapes freehand. Pipe a swirly decoration for the top of the cake. Leave all the ornaments to dry for 24 hours.

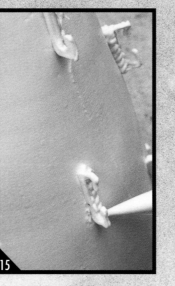

15 Stick the loops to the cake with a little royal icing. Begin at the base of the cake and work upwards in a spiral motion, spacing the loops about 6 inches apart. Strengthen the loops by piping extra royal icing onto the cake along both side of each loop. Pipe decoration around the base of the cake, then let dry for at least 4 hours.

16 and 17 Starting at the base of the cake, carefully thread ribbon through the royal icing loops, loosely up the side of the cake.

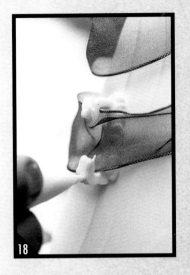

18 To fix the ornaments to the loops, pipe a little royal icing to the edges of the loops.

19 Pipe a little royal icing to the back of each ornament before gently sticking it onto its loop.

20 Place each ornament into the desired position, lightly pressing so that it bonds to the fitting.

21 Using a scissor blade, make a groove on the top of the cake.

22 Pipe a dot of royal icing onto the top of the cake and carefully position the swirly ornament so that it sits in the groove on top.

23 Pipe clusters of dots over the cake, spiralling upwards like a pattern of air bubbles in water.

24 Fill any spaces in the clusters with more dots, if necessary.

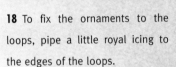

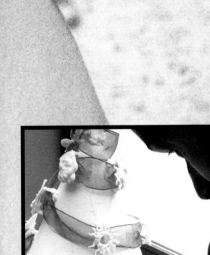

templates

Cut out templates to use for the designs in the book, from cardboard or from a sheet of thin plastic. If you use plastic, you will be able to use the templates again and again. To make larger or smaller designs than those shown here, simply increase or decrease the size of the template, following the shape of the motif.

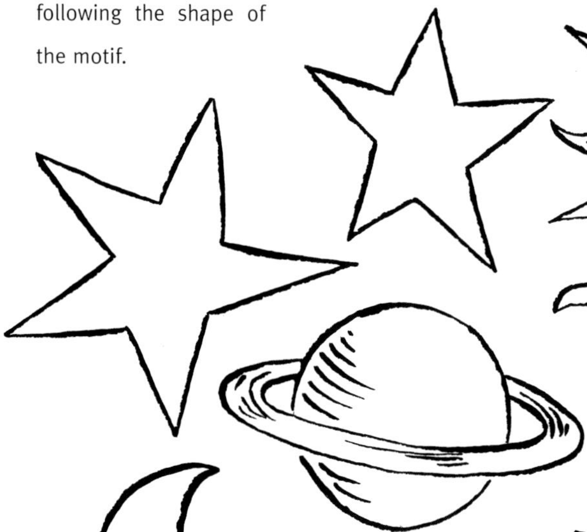

Santas, page 28

suns, stars, and Saturns from
Chocolate Celebration Cake, page 64

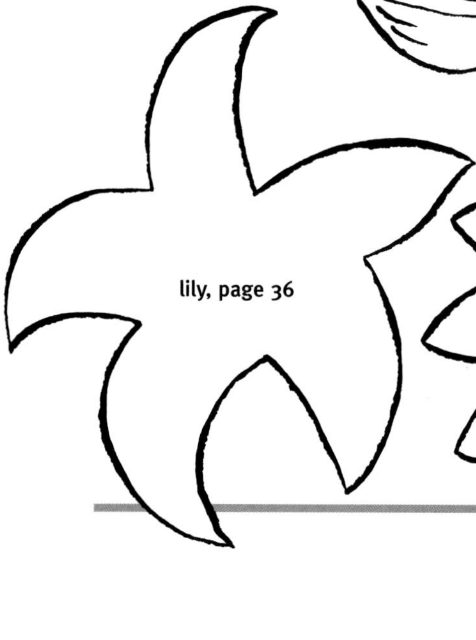

lily, page 36

sunflower, page 37

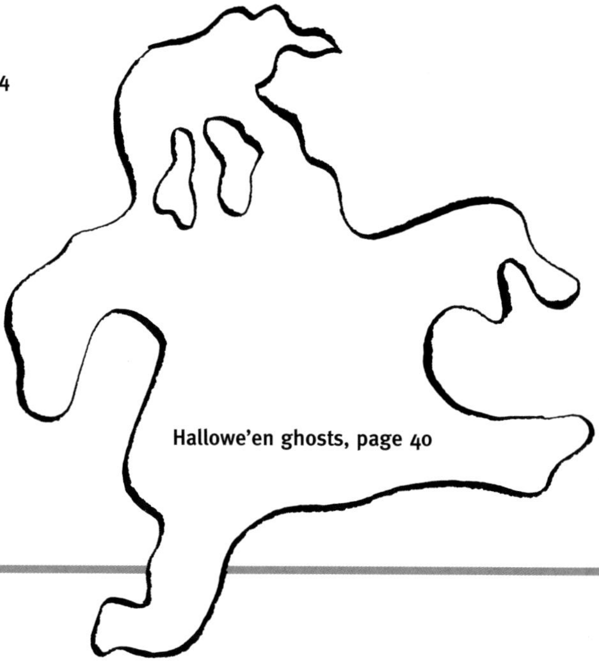

Hallowe'en ghosts, page 40

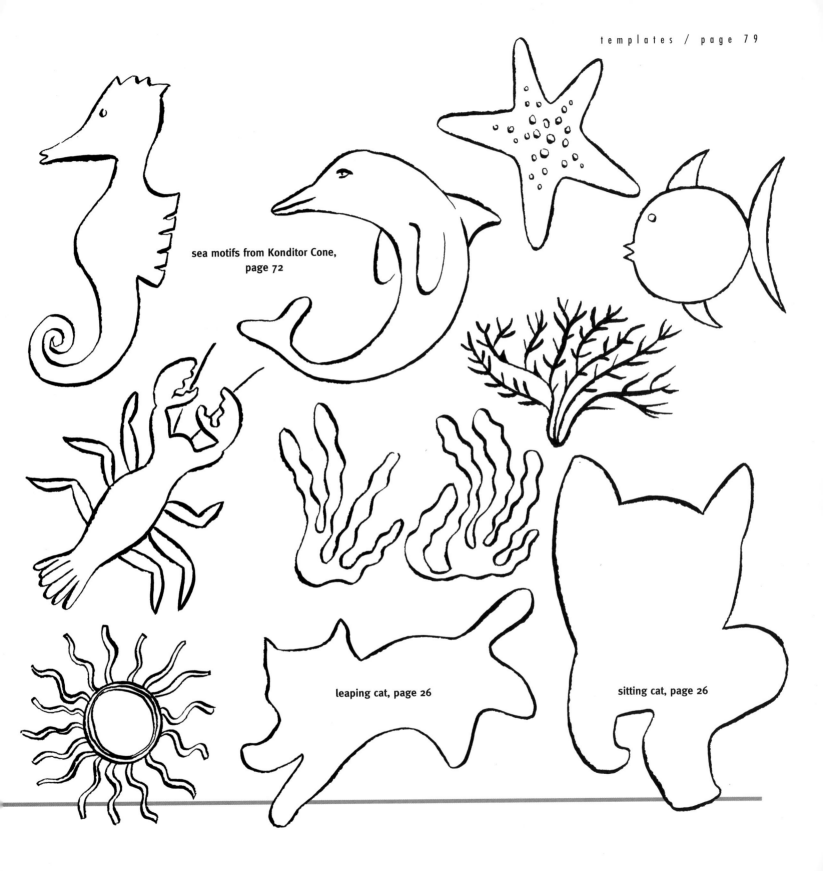

sea motifs from Konditor Cone,
page 72

leaping cat, page 26

sitting cat, page 26

index

conversion charts

Weights and measures have been rounded up or down slightly to make measuring easier.

Volume equivalents:

American	Metric	Imperial
1 teaspoon	5 ml	
1 tablespoon	15 ml	
¼ cup	60 ml	2 fl.oz.
⅓ cup	75 ml	2½ fl.oz.
½ cup	125 ml	4 fl.oz.
⅔ cup	150 ml	5 fl.oz. (¼ pint)
¾ cup	175 ml	6 fl.oz.
1 cup	250 ml	8 fl.oz.

Weight equivalents: Measurements:

Imperial	Metric	Inches	Cm
1 oz.	25 g	¼ inch	5 mm
2 oz.	50 g	½ inch	1 cm
3 oz.	75 g	¾ inch	1.5 cm
4 oz.	125 g	1 inch	2.5 cm
5 oz.	150 g	2 inches	5 cm
6 oz.	175 g	3 inches	7 cm
7 oz.	200 g	4 inches	10 cm
8 oz. (½ lb.)	250 g	5 inches	12 cm
9 oz.	275 g	6 inches	15 cm
10 oz.	300 g	7 inches	18 cm
11 oz.	325 g	8 inches	20 cm
12 oz.	375 g	9 inches	23 cm
13 oz.	400 g	10 inches	25 cm
14 oz.	425 g	11 inches	28 cm
15 oz.	475 g	12 inches	30 cm
16 oz. (1 lb.)	500 g		
2 1b.	1 kg		

Oven temperatures:

110°C	(225°F)	Gas ¼
120°C	(250°F)	Gas ½
140°C	(275°F)	Gas 1
150°C	(300°F)	Gas 2
160°C	(325°F)	Gas 3
180°C	(350°F)	Gas 4
190°C	(375°F)	Gas 5
200°C	(400°F)	Gas 6
220°C	(425°F)	Gas 7
230°C	(450°F)	Gas 8
240°C	(475°F)	Gas 9